Mastering Stress Management: The Art of Setting Realistic Goals

Jakob Nielsen

Copyright © [2023]

Title: Mastering Stress Management: The Art of Setting Realistic Goals

Author's: Jakob Nielsen.

All rights reserved. No part of this publication may be reproduced, stored in a retrieval system, or transmitted in any form or by any means, electronic, mechanical, photocopying, recording, or otherwise, without the prior written permission of the publisher or author, except in the case of brief quotations embodied in critical reviews and certain other non-commercial uses permitted by copyright law.

This book was printed and published by [Publisher's: Jakob Nielsen] in [2023]

ISBN:

TABLE OF COJNTENTS

Chapter 1: Understanding Stress Management   06

The Importance of Stress Management

Common Causes of Stress

The Effects of Stress on Mental and Physical Health

Chapter 2: The Benefits of Setting Realistic Goals   12

How Goals Contribute to Stress Management

The Link Between Goals and Motivation

Setting Realistic Goals for Long-Term Success

Chapter 3: Assessing Your Current Situation   18

Identifying Stress Triggers

Evaluating Your Stress Levels

Recognizing Areas of Improvement

Chapter 4: Setting Effective Goals for Stress Management 24

The SMART Goal-Setting Framework

Determining Short-Term and Long-Term Goals

Prioritizing Goals for Maximum Impact

Chapter 5: Breaking Down Goals into Actionable Steps 30

Creating an Action Plan

Establishing Milestones for Progress

Dealing with Potential Obstacles

Chapter 6: Tracking Progress and Adjusting Goals 36

Monitoring Your Progress

Celebrating Achievements

Modifying Goals as Needed

Chapter 7: Overcoming Challenges and Staying Motivated 42

Dealing with Procrastination and Self-Doubt

Finding Support Systems

Maintaining a Positive Mindset

Chapter 8: Building Resilience and Stress Coping Strategies 48

Developing Resilience Techniques

Implementing Stress Coping Strategies

Seeking Professional Help When Needed

Chapter 9: Balancing Goals and Self-Care 54

The Importance of Self-Care in Stress Management

Incorporating Self-Care Activities into Daily Routine

Finding a Healthy Balance Between Goals and Well-being

Chapter 10: Sustaining Long-Term Success in Stress Management 60

Maintaining Consistency in Goal-Setting and Stress Management Practices

Evaluating and Adjusting Goals Over Time

Celebrating and Reflecting on Personal Growth

Conclusion: Embracing a Stress-Free Future 66

Chapter 1: Understanding Stress Management

The Importance of Stress Management

In today's fast-paced and demanding world, stress has become an inevitable part of our lives. Whether you are a student, a working professional, a parent, or just someone trying to navigate through the challenges of daily life, stress can take a toll on your mental and physical well-being. That's why it is crucial to understand the importance of stress management and learn effective strategies to cope with it.

Stress, if left unmanaged, can have detrimental effects on both your physical and mental health. It can lead to chronic illnesses such as high blood pressure, heart disease, and even depression. Moreover, stress negatively impacts your cognitive abilities, making it difficult to concentrate, solve problems, and make rational decisions. It can also affect your relationships, causing conflicts and a general sense of dissatisfaction in your personal and professional life.

Proper stress management is the key to leading a healthy and fulfilling life. It helps you regain control over your emotions, thoughts, and behaviors, allowing you to handle challenging situations with resilience and clarity. By mastering stress management techniques, you can enhance your overall well-being and achieve a greater sense of fulfillment.

One effective strategy for managing stress is setting realistic goals. When you set achievable goals, you create a sense of purpose and direction in your life. This helps alleviate stress by providing you with a clear roadmap to follow, reducing feelings of uncertainty and overwhelm. By breaking down larger goals into smaller, manageable tasks, you can make progress step by step, which boosts your confidence and reduces stress levels.

Another crucial aspect of stress management is self-care. Taking care of yourself both physically and mentally is essential in combating stress. Engaging in activities that promote relaxation and rejuvenation, such as exercise, meditation, and hobbies, can significantly reduce stress levels. Additionally, maintaining a healthy lifestyle through proper nutrition, regular sleep patterns, and a balanced work-life routine can greatly contribute to stress reduction.

In conclusion, stress management is of utmost importance for everyone, regardless of their background or occupation. By understanding the negative impacts of stress and learning effective strategies to manage it, you can improve your overall well-being and lead a more fulfilling life. Setting achievable goals and practicing self-care are key components of stress management that can help you navigate through life's challenges with resilience and ease. Remember, mastering stress management is an art that requires dedication, practice, and a commitment to prioritize your mental and physical health.

Common Causes of Stress

In today's fast-paced world, stress has become an inevitable part of our lives. No matter who you are or what you do, stress can affect anyone at any time. It is essential to understand the common causes of stress to effectively manage it and lead a healthier, more fulfilling life.

One of the primary causes of stress is work-related pressure. Whether you have a demanding job or are struggling with unemployment, the stress of meeting deadlines, managing responsibilities, and dealing with difficult colleagues can take a toll on your mental well-being. Financial worries also contribute significantly to stress levels, as the fear of not being able to make ends meet can be overwhelming.

Relationships, both personal and professional, can be another significant source of stress. Conflicts with family members, friends, or co-workers can lead to feelings of frustration, anger, and anxiety. The pressure to maintain healthy relationships and meet the expectations of others can be burdensome, leading to stress.

Health-related concerns can also trigger stress. Chronic illnesses, physical injuries, or even the fear of falling sick can create a constant state of worry and anxiety. Additionally, poor lifestyle choices such as an unhealthy diet, lack of exercise, and inadequate sleep can contribute to stress levels, as these factors impact overall well-being.

Another common cause of stress is the inability to manage time effectively. Feeling overwhelmed by a seemingly never-ending to-do list can leave you feeling stressed and anxious. Poor time management skills can lead to missed deadlines, increased workload, and a sense of being constantly in catch-up mode.

Furthermore, life transitions and significant events can also cause stress. Whether it's moving to a new city, starting a new job, getting married, or experiencing the loss of a loved one, these changes can disrupt our routine and stability, leading to heightened stress levels.

Recognizing these common causes of stress is the first step toward effective stress management. By understanding the triggers, you can develop coping strategies and set realistic goals to minimize stress in your life. Remember, stress is a normal part of life, but how you respond to it can make all the difference.

In the following chapters of "Mastering Stress Management: The Art of Setting Realistic Goals," we will explore various techniques and strategies to help you effectively manage stress and set achievable goals. By mastering these skills, you can cultivate a healthier, more balanced lifestyle and unlock your full potential.

The Effects of Stress on Mental and Physical Health

Stress has become an inevitable part of our lives, affecting people of all ages and backgrounds. Whether you are a student, a working professional, or a homemaker, stress can have a profound impact on your mental and physical well-being. In this subchapter, we will delve into the effects of stress on both aspects of health and discuss strategies for managing and reducing stress.

Mental Health:
Stress can take a toll on your mental health, leading to a range of emotional and psychological issues. Prolonged exposure to stress can cause anxiety, depression, irritability, and mood swings. It can disrupt your sleep patterns, making it difficult to fall asleep or stay asleep, leading to chronic fatigue and decreased cognitive function. Additionally, stress can impair your ability to concentrate, make decisions, and solve problems effectively. It can also exacerbate existing mental health conditions, such as bipolar disorder or post-traumatic stress disorder (PTSD).

Physical Health:
Stress doesn't just affect your mind; it also has a significant impact on your physical health. When you are under stress, your body releases cortisol, commonly known as the stress hormone. Increased levels of cortisol can lead to a weakened immune system, making you more susceptible to illnesses and infections. Stress can also disrupt your digestive system, leading to stomachaches, indigestion, and even irritable bowel syndrome (IBS). Additionally, chronic stress can contribute to cardiovascular problems, such as high blood pressure,

heart disease, and stroke. It can also manifest in physical symptoms like headaches, muscle tension, and chronic pain.

Managing and Reducing Stress: Fortunately, there are several strategies you can employ to manage and reduce stress. One of the most effective techniques is setting realistic and achievable goals. By breaking down larger tasks into smaller, more manageable steps, you can alleviate the overwhelming feeling that often accompanies stress. Additionally, practicing relaxation techniques, such as deep breathing exercises, meditation, and yoga, can help calm your mind and reduce stress levels. Engaging in regular physical exercise, maintaining a healthy diet, and getting sufficient sleep are also crucial in managing stress. Furthermore, seeking support from friends, family, or a professional counselor can provide you with valuable guidance and assistance in navigating stressful situations.

Remember, stress is a natural response to life's challenges, but prolonged exposure to stress can have detrimental effects on your mental and physical health. By understanding the impact of stress and implementing effective stress management techniques, you can lead a healthier and more balanced life.

Chapter 2: The Benefits of Setting Realistic Goals

How Goals Contribute to Stress Management

Setting goals is a fundamental aspect of human nature. We all have dreams, aspirations, and things we want to achieve in life. However, the process of goal setting can often lead to stress and anxiety if not approached correctly. In this subchapter, we will explore how goals can actually contribute to stress management when done properly.

One of the key ways in which goals contribute to stress management is by providing a sense of direction and purpose. When we have clear goals in mind, we are better able to prioritize our actions and make decisions that align with our objectives. This clarity helps to reduce stress by eliminating the uncertainty and indecisiveness that often plagues our daily lives.

Furthermore, setting achievable goals allows us to break down larger tasks into smaller, more manageable steps. By doing so, we avoid feeling overwhelmed and can focus on one task at a time. This approach not only enhances productivity but also minimizes stress levels as we feel a sense of accomplishment with each smaller goal achieved.

In addition, setting realistic goals encourages us to develop effective time management skills. When we have a clear understanding of what needs to be done and by when, we can allocate our time more efficiently. This decreases the likelihood of procrastination and the resulting stress that comes from rushing to meet deadlines.

Moreover, goals serve as a motivator and a source of inspiration. When we have something to strive for, we are more likely to stay focused and driven. This intrinsic motivation helps us overcome obstacles and setbacks, reducing stress caused by self-doubt or lack of progress.

Finally, the process of setting goals allows for self-reflection and personal growth. As we evaluate our strengths, weaknesses, and areas for improvement, we gain a better understanding of ourselves. By setting goals that challenge us but are still within reach, we foster a sense of self-confidence and self-efficacy. This self-assurance helps to alleviate stress by promoting a positive mindset and belief in our abilities.

In conclusion, goal setting is an essential tool for stress management. By providing a sense of direction, breaking down tasks, improving time management, motivating us, and fostering personal growth, goals contribute to a more balanced and fulfilling life. Whether you are a student, a professional, or a homemaker, mastering the art of setting realistic goals will help you manage stress and achieve success in all areas of your life.

The Link Between Goals and Motivation

Setting goals is a vital step in achieving success and personal growth. Goals provide us with direction and purpose, giving us something to strive for. However, merely setting goals is not enough; we must also understand the link between goals and motivation.

Motivation is the driving force behind our actions and behaviors. It is what keeps us going when faced with challenges and obstacles. Without motivation, it becomes difficult to stay focused and committed to our goals. Therefore, understanding how goals and motivation are interconnected is crucial to achieving success.

Goals act as a catalyst for motivation. When we set specific, measurable, achievable, relevant, and time-bound (SMART) goals, we create a roadmap for success. These goals provide us with a clear vision of what we want to achieve and help us stay motivated along the way.

When we have a well-defined goal, it stimulates our brain's reward system. This system releases chemicals such as dopamine, a neurotransmitter associated with pleasure and motivation. As we make progress towards our goals, we experience a sense of accomplishment, which further fuels our motivation.

Moreover, goals give us a sense of purpose. They provide us with a reason to get out of bed each morning and take action. Without goals, we may find ourselves drifting aimlessly, lacking the drive and determination necessary to achieve our dreams. When we have a clear purpose, we are more likely to stay motivated and overcome obstacles that come our way.

Setting achievable goals is also crucial for maintaining motivation. If our goals are too lofty or unrealistic, we may become discouraged and lose motivation. On the other hand, setting small, attainable goals allows us to experience success regularly, boosting our motivation to keep going.

To enhance motivation, it is essential to periodically review and revise our goals. As we progress and grow, our aspirations may change, and it is vital to ensure our goals align with our current desires and values. By regularly reassessing our goals, we can maintain motivation and stay on the path towards success.

In conclusion, goals and motivation are closely intertwined. Setting realistic and achievable goals provides us with direction and purpose, stimulating our brain's reward system and fueling our motivation. By understanding the link between goals and motivation, we can harness this powerful connection to achieve our dreams and live a fulfilling life.

Setting Realistic Goals for Long-Term Success

In today's fast-paced world, setting realistic goals is essential for long-term success. Whether you are a student, a professional, an entrepreneur, or anyone striving to achieve their dreams, learning how to set achievable goals is crucial. In this subchapter, we will explore the art of setting realistic goals and provide practical tips for success.

When it comes to setting goals, it is important to start by understanding your own capabilities and limitations. Each person is unique, with different skills, resources, and circumstances. Acknowledging these factors will help you set goals that are challenging yet within reach. It is crucial to avoid setting goals that are too ambitious or unrealistic, as they can lead to frustration and demotivation.

To begin, take the time to identify your long-term vision and break it down into smaller, manageable goals. By setting achievable milestones, you can measure your progress and stay motivated throughout your journey. Remember to be specific when defining your goals – the more precise they are, the easier it will be to track your progress and make adjustments along the way.

One key aspect of setting realistic goals is to ensure they are aligned with your values and priorities. Ask yourself what truly matters to you and how your goals align with these values. This will provide a sense of purpose and make you more committed to achieving them.

It is also important to set deadlines for your goals. Without a deadline, it is easy to procrastinate and lose focus. However, make sure the deadlines are reasonable and flexible, allowing room for unexpected challenges or opportunities.

In addition to these principles, it is helpful to break your goals into smaller, actionable steps. This will make them less overwhelming and more attainable. Celebrate each milestone achieved, as it will provide a sense of accomplishment and motivate you to continue moving forward.

Lastly, remember that setbacks and obstacles are inevitable. Instead of being discouraged, view them as opportunities for growth and learning. Adjust your goals if necessary, but never give up on your long-term vision.

Setting realistic goals for long-term success is a valuable skill that can transform your life. By understanding your capabilities, aligning your goals with your values, setting deadlines, breaking them into actionable steps, and embracing setbacks, you will be well on your way to achieving what you once thought was impossible. Start today, and let your journey towards success begin!

Chapter 3: Assessing Your Current Situation

Identifying Stress Triggers

In the fast-paced and demanding world we live in, stress has become an inevitable part of our lives. It affects people from all walks of life, regardless of age, profession, or background. However, the key to managing stress lies in understanding its root causes. By identifying our stress triggers, we can take proactive steps to reduce their impact on our lives and ultimately achieve a healthier, more balanced state of being.

The first step in identifying stress triggers is self-reflection. Take a moment to reflect on situations or circumstances that consistently make you feel overwhelmed or anxious. Is it a particular task at work, a certain type of interaction with others, or maybe a recurring life event? By recognizing patterns, we can gain valuable insights into the specific triggers that contribute to our stress levels.

Another useful technique is keeping a stress journal. Document your daily experiences, emotions, and any situations that elicit stress. By recording these details, you can start to identify common themes or patterns that emerge. Perhaps you notice that you always feel stressed when deadlines are approaching, or when you have conflicts with a certain individual. This journal can serve as a valuable tool for self-reflection and provide a clearer understanding of your personal stress triggers.

It is also important to pay attention to physical and emotional cues that indicate stress. Do you experience tension in your muscles, headaches, or digestive issues when faced with certain situations? Are you more irritable, fatigued, or have difficulty concentrating during these times? These physical and emotional responses can act as warning signs, alerting you to potential stress triggers.

Additionally, seeking feedback from others can be enlightening. Ask trusted friends, family members, or colleagues if they have noticed any patterns in your behavior during times of stress. They may offer valuable insights that you may not have considered.

Once you have identified your stress triggers, the next step is to develop effective strategies to manage and mitigate their impact. By setting realistic goals, you can address these triggers head-on and create a plan for managing stress in a healthy and sustainable way.

Remember, identifying stress triggers is a personal journey, and what may cause stress for one person may not affect another in the same way. By taking the time to understand your own unique stress triggers, you can gain control over your stress levels and work towards a more balanced and fulfilling life.

Evaluating Your Stress Levels

In order to effectively manage stress and set realistic goals, it is crucial to first evaluate your stress levels. Stress can have a profound impact on our mental and physical well-being, as well as our ability to achieve the goals we set for ourselves. This subchapter will guide you through a self-assessment process to help you gain a better understanding of your stress levels and how they may be affecting your goal-setting endeavors.

Stress manifests differently in each individual, and it is important to recognize the signs and symptoms that indicate high stress levels. These may include irritability, difficulty concentrating, changes in appetite or sleep patterns, increased heart rate, and feelings of overwhelm or anxiety. By being aware of these indicators, you can begin to identify patterns and triggers that contribute to your stress levels.

One effective way to evaluate your stress levels is to keep a stress journal. This involves recording daily events, emotions, and any stressors that arise throughout the day. By maintaining this journal for a few weeks, you can identify recurring sources of stress and gain insight into how they impact your ability to set and achieve goals. Additionally, it can help you recognize any unhealthy coping mechanisms you may be using, such as excessive caffeine consumption or procrastination.

Another valuable tool for evaluating stress levels is the use of stress assessments or questionnaires. These assessments provide a standardized framework to measure your stress levels and identify areas of improvement. They often cover various aspects of life, such as work, relationships, and personal well-being. By completing such assessments, you can gain a clearer picture of your stress levels and identify specific areas that require attention.

Furthermore, it is essential to pay attention to physical symptoms that may be indicative of high stress levels. Chronic headaches, muscle tension, frequent illnesses, and digestive issues are common physical manifestations of stress. By being attuned to your body's signals, you can recognize the impact stress has on your physical health and take proactive measures to address it.

Evaluating your stress levels is a vital step in mastering stress management and setting realistic goals. By gaining awareness of your stressors, triggers, and physical symptoms, you can begin to implement effective stress reduction techniques and make adjustments to your goal-setting strategies. Remember, self-care and stress management are essential components of achieving success and maintaining a balanced and fulfilling life.

Recognizing Areas of Improvement

In the journey towards mastering stress management and setting realistic goals, it is essential to recognize and acknowledge areas that require improvement. The ability to identify these areas allows individuals to develop a focused plan for personal growth and success. No matter who you are or what your goals may be, understanding how to recognize areas of improvement is a crucial skill that can benefit everyone.

Setting achievable goals begins with self-reflection and an honest assessment of one's current strengths and weaknesses. By recognizing areas where improvement is needed, individuals can develop a roadmap for personal development that aligns with their aspirations. This process requires self-awareness and a willingness to step outside of one's comfort zone.

The first step in recognizing areas of improvement is to evaluate your current situation. Take some time to reflect on different aspects of your life such as career, relationships, health, and personal development. Ask yourself questions like, "Am I satisfied with my current level of performance in these areas?" or "What areas do I feel are holding me back from achieving my goals?"

Once you have identified potential areas for improvement, it is crucial to set realistic and actionable goals. Start by breaking down larger goals into smaller, more manageable steps. This approach will help you maintain motivation and track progress along the way. Remember, the key is to set achievable goals that push you outside of your comfort zone but are still within reach.

Seeking feedback from others can also be incredibly valuable in recognizing areas of improvement. Ask trusted friends, family members, or colleagues for their honest opinions and observations. This external perspective can provide valuable insights that may not be apparent to you.

Recognizing areas of improvement is an ongoing process. As you work towards your goals, regularly evaluate and reassess your progress. Celebrate your successes and learn from your setbacks. Remember that personal growth is a lifelong journey, and each step forward is a victory in itself.

In conclusion, recognizing areas of improvement is a vital aspect of mastering stress management and setting realistic goals. It requires self-reflection, goal-setting, and seeking feedback from others. By acknowledging areas that need improvement and taking actionable steps towards personal growth, individuals can unlock their full potential and achieve their aspirations. No matter who you are or what your goals may be, recognizing areas of improvement is a valuable skill that can benefit everyone on their journey towards success.

Chapter 4: Setting Effective Goals for Stress Management

The SMART Goal-Setting Framework

In today's fast-paced world, setting goals has become a crucial aspect of our lives. Whether it's in our personal or professional endeavors, knowing how to set achievable goals is essential for success. The SMART goal-setting framework provides a structured approach that can help individuals set realistic and attainable objectives. By following this framework, you can effectively manage your stress and master the art of goal setting.

SMART is an acronym that stands for Specific, Measurable, Achievable, Relevant, and Time-bound. Each of these elements plays a vital role in creating goals that are both challenging and realistic.

First and foremost, goals must be Specific. By clearly defining what you want to achieve, you provide yourself with a clear direction and focus. Vague goals can often lead to confusion and lack of motivation. Being specific helps you visualize your desired outcome and enables you to create a plan of action.

Next, goals should be Measurable. This means that you need to establish clear criteria to measure your progress. By setting measurable goals, you can track your achievements and stay motivated throughout the journey. It also allows you to identify any adjustments that may be required along the way.

Achievable goals are those that are within your reach and capabilities. While it's important to challenge yourself, setting unattainable goals can lead to frustration and demotivation. Assess your resources, skills, and limitations to ensure that your goals are realistic and can be accomplished with the available means.

Relevance is another crucial aspect of goal setting. Your goals should align with your values, passions, and long-term objectives. When your goals are relevant to your overall aspirations, you are more likely to stay committed and dedicated to achieving them.

Lastly, goals need to be Time-bound. Set specific deadlines or timeframes to keep yourself accountable and motivated. By giving yourself a timeline, you create a sense of urgency and prevent procrastination. Breaking your goals into smaller milestones with deadlines can also help you stay on track and maintain momentum.

The SMART goal-setting framework is a powerful tool that can assist anyone in setting achievable goals. Whether you are a student, professional, or someone pursuing personal growth, understanding and implementing this framework can greatly enhance your ability to manage stress and attain success. So, take the time to apply the SMART principles to your goal-setting process and watch your dreams turn into reality. Remember, you have the power to master stress management through realistic and well-defined goals.

Determining Short-Term and Long-Term Goals

Setting goals is an essential aspect of personal and professional development. Whether you are a student, a working professional, or a stay-at-home parent, having clear objectives can help you stay focused and motivated. However, setting realistic goals can be a daunting task for many. In this subchapter, we will explore the art of determining short-term and long-term goals, providing you with practical strategies to set achievable objectives.

Short-term goals are those that can be accomplished within a relatively short period, typically ranging from a few days to a few months. These goals act as stepping stones towards your long-term objectives. When determining short-term goals, it is crucial to consider your current circumstances and available resources. Ask yourself: What can I realistically achieve in the near future? How can I align these goals with my long-term aspirations?

Long-term goals, on the other hand, are those that require more time and effort to accomplish. They often span several months or even years. When determining long-term goals, it is essential to envision your desired future and think about the steps necessary to reach that point. Consider what you want to achieve in your career, relationships, health, and personal growth. Break down these long-term goals into smaller, manageable milestones that you can work towards in the short-term.

To set achievable goals, it is crucial to follow the SMART criteria. Ensure that your goals are Specific, Measurable, Attainable, Relevant, and Time-bound. By being specific and measurable, you can clearly define what you want to achieve and track your progress effectively. Make sure your goals are attainable and realistic, ensuring that they are within your capabilities and available resources. They should also be relevant to your overall aspirations and values. Lastly, set a deadline for each goal to create a sense of urgency and keep you motivated.

Remember to regularly review and adjust your goals as circumstances change. Flexibility is essential in goal-setting, as it allows you to adapt to new opportunities or challenges that may arise. Celebrate your achievements along the way, as this will help you stay motivated and reinforce your commitment to your goals.

In conclusion, determining short-term and long-term goals is a crucial aspect of personal and professional growth. By following the SMART criteria and regularly reviewing and adjusting your objectives, you can set achievable goals that align with your aspirations. Remember, setting realistic goals takes time and practice, so be patient with yourself. With dedication and perseverance, you can master the art of setting realistic goals and achieve success in all areas of your life.

Prioritizing Goals for Maximum Impact

Setting goals is an essential aspect of personal and professional growth. However, without effective prioritization, even the most well-intentioned goals can become overwhelming and ultimately unachievable. In this subchapter, we will explore the art of prioritizing goals for maximum impact, providing you with practical strategies to set achievable goals and ensure long-term success.

1. Define Your Values: Before embarking on goal-setting, it is crucial to identify your core values. Understanding what truly matters to you will help you prioritize goals that align with your personal beliefs and aspirations. By focusing on goals that resonate with your values, you will increase your motivation and commitment to achieve them.

2. Evaluate Urgency and Importance: Not all goals hold equal weight. To prioritize effectively, assess the urgency and importance of each goal. Urgent goals require immediate attention, while important goals contribute to your long-term vision. By categorizing goals based on these criteria, you can allocate your time and resources accordingly.

3. Consider Long-Term Impact: While short-term goals may seem enticing, it is essential to consider their long-term impact. Will achieving this goal contribute to your overall growth and well-being? Prioritize goals that have a lasting, positive effect on your life and align with your long-term vision.

4. Break Goals into Manageable Steps: Overwhelming goals can lead to stress and demotivation. To mitigate this, break larger goals into smaller, manageable steps. By focusing on one step at a time, you can

maintain your momentum and progressively work towards your larger objective.

5. Utilize the SMART Framework: The SMART framework (Specific, Measurable, Achievable, Relevant, Time-bound) is a powerful tool for goal-setting. Ensure your goals are specific, measurable, realistic, and time-bound. This framework provides clarity, enabling you to prioritize goals based on their achievability and alignment with your overall objectives.

6. Flexibility and Adaptability: Priorities can shift as circumstances change, and it is crucial to remain flexible and adaptable. Regularly reassess your goals and adjust your priorities accordingly. By being open to change, you can ensure your efforts are directed towards goals that have the most significant impact in the present moment.

Remember, effective goal prioritization is an ongoing process. As you grow and evolve, so will your goals. By consistently practicing these strategies, you will master the art of setting realistic and achievable goals, leading to personal and professional fulfillment.

Whether you are a student, professional, or someone seeking personal growth, prioritizing goals for maximum impact is a fundamental skill. By setting clear priorities, breaking goals into manageable steps, and regularly reassessing your objectives, you can ensure that your efforts are channeled towards the most important and impactful goals. Start prioritizing today and unlock your true potential!

Chapter 5: Breaking Down Goals into Actionable Steps

Creating an Action Plan

In the journey towards mastering stress management, one crucial aspect is learning how to set realistic and achievable goals. Without a clear sense of direction and a plan in place, we can easily find ourselves overwhelmed and stressed. That's where creating an action plan comes into play.

An action plan is a strategic roadmap that outlines the specific steps needed to accomplish a goal. It breaks down the larger goal into smaller, manageable tasks, making it easier to track progress and stay motivated. Whether you're aiming to improve your time management skills, increase productivity, or enhance your overall well-being, following these steps will help you create an effective action plan:

1. Define your goal: Begin by clearly defining your objective. Be specific and ensure that your goal is measurable and attainable. For example, instead of stating, "I want to be less stressed," specify, "I will engage in daily stress-relief activities for at least 30 minutes."

2. Break it down: Once you have your main goal, break it down into smaller tasks. These should be bite-sized actions that you can easily accomplish within a set timeframe. For instance, if your goal is to exercise more, your tasks could include researching different workout routines, scheduling gym sessions, and purchasing workout attire.

3. Set deadlines: Assign deadlines to each task to create a sense of urgency and prevent procrastination. Be realistic with your timeframes, taking into consideration other commitments and potential obstacles that may arise.

4. Prioritize tasks: Determine which tasks are most important and prioritize them accordingly. This will ensure that you tackle the most crucial aspects first and maintain focus throughout the process.

5. Track progress: Regularly monitor your progress to stay motivated and make adjustments as needed. Keep a journal or use a tracking app to record completed tasks, milestones achieved, and any challenges encountered. Celebrate your victories along the way to boost your confidence and maintain momentum.

6. Seek support: Don't be afraid to ask for help or seek support from friends, family, or professionals. Having someone to hold you accountable and provide guidance can greatly enhance your chances of success.

Remember, creating an action plan is just the first step. It's essential to maintain discipline, stay committed, and adapt as circumstances change. By following this process, you'll be well on your way to setting achievable goals and mastering stress management.

Establishing Milestones for Progress

In the journey towards achieving our goals, it is crucial to establish milestones that serve as markers of progress. These milestones act as guideposts that help us stay on track, measure our achievements, and maintain motivation throughout the process. In this subchapter, we will explore the art of setting realistic milestones and how they contribute to effective stress management.

Setting achievable goals is an essential skill for every individual, regardless of their background or aspirations. Whether you are a student, a professional, an entrepreneur, or a homemaker, learning how to set realistic goals is the key to unlocking your full potential. But merely setting goals is not enough; breaking them down into manageable milestones is equally important.

Milestones are like stepping stones that bridge the gap between where you are now and where you want to be. By breaking down your larger goals into smaller, more attainable milestones, you create a roadmap that allows you to track progress and celebrate achievements along the way. This incremental approach not only helps to prevent overwhelm but also boosts confidence and motivation.

To set effective milestones, start by clearly defining your larger goal. What is it that you want to achieve? Be specific and ensure your goal is measurable. Once you have a clear objective in mind, identify the smaller tasks or steps that will lead you towards that goal. These steps become your milestones.

It is essential to set milestones that are challenging yet realistic. They should push you out of your comfort zone, but not be so overwhelming that they become unachievable. Each milestone should be time-bound, allowing you to track your progress and evaluate whether you are on track or need to adjust your strategy.

Regularly reviewing and adjusting your milestones is crucial to stay on course. As you progress, you may encounter unexpected obstacles or opportunities that require adaptation. By regularly assessing your milestones, you can make necessary adjustments and keep moving forward.

Remember, the journey towards achieving your goals is not a straight path. It is filled with twists and turns, highs and lows. However, by establishing milestones for progress, you can navigate these challenges with greater ease and resilience. Embrace the power of milestones, and you will find yourself mastering stress management while achieving your dreams.

Dealing with Potential Obstacles

Setting realistic goals is a crucial step towards achieving success and personal fulfillment. However, along the journey of goal attainment, it is inevitable to encounter various obstacles that can hinder progress and create stress. In this subchapter, we will explore effective strategies for dealing with potential obstacles, ensuring that you stay on track and maintain a positive mindset throughout your goal-setting journey.

1. Identify potential obstacles: The first step in overcoming obstacles is to be aware of them. Take some time to identify potential challenges that may arise along the way. These obstacles can be external, such as financial constraints or lack of resources, or internal, such as self-doubt or fear of failure. By recognizing and acknowledging these hurdles, you can better prepare yourself to confront and overcome them.

2. Develop a problem-solving mindset: Instead of viewing obstacles as roadblocks, reframe them as opportunities for growth and learning. Adopt a problem-solving mindset that focuses on finding solutions rather than dwelling on the problems themselves. Embrace challenges as chances to develop resilience and creativity, and believe in your ability to find innovative ways to overcome any obstacle.

3. Seek support and guidance: Don't be afraid to ask for help when needed. Reach out to mentors, friends, or colleagues who have faced similar challenges and can offer guidance and support. Surround yourself with a network of positive and encouraging individuals who can provide valuable insights and alternative perspectives, helping you navigate through obstacles more effectively.

4. Break it down: Sometimes, obstacles can appear overwhelming and insurmountable. To prevent feeling overwhelmed, break down your goals into smaller, more manageable tasks. By focusing on one step at a time, you can maintain a sense of progress and build momentum, which will ultimately propel you forward despite any obstacles you may encounter.

5. Practice self-care: Dealing with obstacles can be mentally and emotionally draining. It is crucial to prioritize self-care to maintain your overall well-being. Engage in activities that bring you joy and relaxation, such as exercise, meditation, or spending time with loved ones. Taking care of yourself will replenish your energy and mental resilience, enabling you to tackle obstacles with a clear and focused mind.

Remember, obstacles are an integral part of the goal-setting journey. Embrace them as opportunities for growth, and utilize the strategies mentioned above to overcome them. With a problem-solving mindset, a supportive network, and a commitment to self-care, you will be well-equipped to navigate through any obstacles that come your way and achieve your realistic goals.

Chapter 6: Tracking Progress and Adjusting Goals

Monitoring Your Progress

In the journey towards achieving our goals, it is crucial to monitor our progress regularly. Monitoring allows us to assess our performance, make necessary adjustments, and stay motivated throughout the process. In this subchapter, we will explore the importance of monitoring your progress and provide valuable tips on how to effectively track your goals.

Why is monitoring your progress essential? Simply put, it helps you stay on track. By regularly assessing your progress, you can identify any deviations from your original plan and take appropriate action. This ensures that you remain focused and committed to your goals. Additionally, monitoring allows you to celebrate your achievements and provides a sense of accomplishment, which boosts motivation and confidence.

To effectively monitor your progress, start by setting specific milestones or checkpoints. These smaller, attainable goals act as indicators of your progress towards the larger goal. They provide a clear framework for assessing your performance and help you stay motivated throughout the process. Break down your goal into smaller, manageable tasks and set deadlines for each milestone.

Next, establish a monitoring system that works for you. This could be a simple checklist, a progress chart, or even a digital app. The key is to choose a method that is easy to use and provides you with a clear overview of your progress. Regularly update your monitoring system and make notes of any challenges or setbacks you encounter along the way. These notes will help you identify patterns and make necessary adjustments to your approach.

In addition to tracking your progress, it is essential to regularly evaluate your goals. Are your goals still relevant? Have your priorities shifted? Evaluating your goals allows you to adapt and modify them as needed, ensuring they remain achievable and aligned with your current aspirations.

Finally, don't forget to celebrate your achievements along the way. Acknowledge your milestones and reward yourself for your hard work and dedication. Celebrating your achievements boosts your motivation and provides you with the energy to continue pursuing your goals.

Monitoring your progress is a vital component of setting and achieving realistic goals. By regularly assessing your performance, adapting your approach, and celebrating your achievements, you can stay on track and maximize your chances of success. Remember, the journey towards your goals is just as important as reaching the destination.

Celebrating Achievements

Subchapter: Celebrating Achievements

In the journey of mastering stress management and setting realistic goals, it is essential to acknowledge and celebrate our achievements along the way. Celebrating our accomplishments not only boosts our self-confidence but also motivates us to continue striving for success. This subchapter will explore the importance of celebrating achievements and provide practical tips on how to effectively celebrate and appreciate our progress.

Every one of us faces various challenges and obstacles while working towards our goals. It is easy to get caught up in the pursuit of perfection and overlook the smaller milestones that lead us to our ultimate objective. However, by taking the time to celebrate these accomplishments, we create a positive cycle of motivation and success.

Recognizing and celebrating achievements allows us to reflect on our progress and the efforts we have invested. It is a reminder of how far we have come and the obstacles we have overcome. This self-reflection helps build self-esteem, resilience, and a positive mindset, which are all essential elements in achieving long-term success.

To effectively celebrate achievements, it is crucial to set realistic and measurable goals from the start. Breaking down our larger objectives into smaller, manageable tasks allows us to celebrate milestones along the way. Each completed task becomes a cause for celebration, reinforcing our belief in our abilities and propelling us forward.

Celebrations need not be grand or extravagant. Simple acts of self-appreciation, such as treating yourself to a favorite meal, indulging in a spa day, or spending quality time with loved ones, can be incredibly rewarding. The key is to acknowledge and reward ourselves for the hard work and dedication we have put into reaching our goals.

Furthermore, sharing our achievements with others can enhance the celebration. Sharing our successes with friends, family, or mentors not only allows us to bask in the joy of our accomplishments but also inspires and motivates others. By celebrating together, we create a supportive network that encourages personal growth and success.

In conclusion, celebrating achievements is an integral part of the goal-setting process. It provides us with the necessary motivation, self-confidence, and resilience to continue pursuing our goals. By setting realistic goals, breaking them down into manageable tasks, and acknowledging each milestone along the way, we create a positive cycle of success. So, take a moment to celebrate your achievements and let them propel you towards even greater accomplishments in the future.

Modifying Goals as Needed

In the journey towards achieving our goals, it is essential to recognize that the path may not always be smooth and straightforward. Life is unpredictable, and circumstances can change in an instant. It is in these moments that we must learn to adapt and modify our goals as needed. This subchapter aims to provide valuable insights into the art of modifying goals, ensuring that we continue to set realistic and achievable targets.

One of the first things to understand is that modifying goals does not equate to giving up or admitting defeat. Instead, it is a sign of resilience and adaptability. As circumstances change, so must our goals. By being open to modifying our goals, we acknowledge the reality of our situation and set ourselves up for success, even in the face of challenges.

To effectively modify goals, it is crucial to regularly assess and evaluate our progress. This involves taking a step back and objectively analyzing our current situation. Are we making the desired progress? Are there any external factors that are hindering our path to success? By honestly answering these questions, we gain clarity and can identify areas where modifications may be necessary.

Flexibility is another key aspect of modifying goals. It is important to understand that rigidity can often lead to frustration and disappointment. Instead, we should be open to adjusting our goals as new information becomes available or circumstances change. This flexibility allows us to adapt our strategies and create new pathways towards achieving our objectives.

Furthermore, seeking support and guidance from others can significantly aid in modifying goals. Surrounding ourselves with a network of mentors, coaches, or even supportive friends can provide fresh perspectives and valuable insights. They can help us identify potential roadblocks and suggest alternative approaches or modifications that we may not have considered on our own.

Ultimately, the art of modifying goals requires a growth mindset. It involves embracing challenges as opportunities for growth and recognizing that setbacks are temporary. By continually reassessing our goals and adapting them as needed, we ensure that we remain on a realistic and achievable path towards success.

In conclusion, modifying goals is a necessary skill in the art of setting realistic and achievable targets. By being open to change, regularly assessing progress, maintaining flexibility, and seeking support, we can navigate through life's uncertainties and continue to make progress towards our goals. Remember, the ability to modify goals is not a sign of weakness but a testament to our resilience and determination to succeed.

Chapter 7: Overcoming Challenges and Staying Motivated

Dealing with Procrastination and Self-Doubt

Procrastination and self-doubt are two common obstacles that hinder us from achieving our goals and living a fulfilling life. In this subchapter, we will explore effective strategies to overcome these challenges and cultivate a mindset of success.

Procrastination is the act of delaying or postponing tasks, often leading to increased stress and missed opportunities. It is a habit that many people struggle with, regardless of age or profession. Whether it's putting off a work project, avoiding exercise, or delaying personal growth, procrastination can be detrimental to our overall well-being.

To tackle procrastination, it is crucial to understand its root causes. Often, it stems from fear of failure, perfectionism, or simply feeling overwhelmed by the task at hand. By recognizing these underlying factors, we can begin to address them head-on.

One effective technique is to break tasks into smaller, more manageable steps. This approach not only makes the task seem less daunting but also provides a sense of progress and accomplishment along the way. Additionally, setting specific deadlines and creating a schedule can help maintain focus and accountability.

Self-doubt, on the other hand, is a common emotional barrier that prevents us from setting and achieving realistic goals. It often manifests as negative self-talk, questioning our abilities or worthiness.

Overcoming self-doubt requires a shift in mindset and a commitment to self-compassion.

One powerful strategy is reframing negative thoughts into positive affirmations. Instead of dwelling on self-criticism, consciously choose to replace those thoughts with statements that promote self-belief and confidence. Surround yourself with supportive and encouraging individuals who uplift and inspire you.

Another helpful technique is to keep a gratitude journal. By regularly reflecting on the things you are grateful for, you can shift your focus from self-doubt to appreciation and self-empowerment. Celebrate your successes, no matter how small, and use them as evidence of your capabilities.

In conclusion, overcoming procrastination and self-doubt is essential for setting and achieving realistic goals. By breaking tasks into manageable steps, setting deadlines, and creating a schedule, we can combat procrastination. Additionally, reframing negative thoughts, surrounding ourselves with positivity, and practicing gratitude can help conquer self-doubt. Remember, everyone faces these challenges at some point, but with the right tools and mindset, you can overcome them and achieve your dreams.

Finding Support Systems

In our journey towards mastering stress management and setting realistic goals, one crucial aspect that often gets overlooked is the importance of finding support systems. We live in a fast-paced world where expectations and pressures can quickly overwhelm us. However, with the right support, we can navigate these challenges and achieve our desired goals.

Support systems come in various forms, and it is essential to identify the ones that work best for you. They can consist of family, friends, mentors, or even professional networks. The purpose of a support system is to provide guidance, encouragement, and a safe space for you to share your thoughts and concerns.

One of the key benefits of having a support system is the opportunity to gain different perspectives. When we are solely focused on our goals, it is easy to become trapped in our own thoughts and limitations. However, by seeking advice from others, we can gain fresh insights and innovative solutions. They can help us see blind spots or potential obstacles we might have missed, making our goals more achievable.

Another advantage of having a support system is the emotional support they provide. Setting realistic goals can be challenging, and setbacks and failures are inevitable. During these times, having someone who understands your struggles and can offer empathy and encouragement can be invaluable. They can remind you of your strengths, help you regain confidence, and motivate you to keep pushing forward.

Support systems also offer accountability, which is crucial when setting achievable goals. When we share our goals with others, we create a sense of responsibility to follow through. Accountability partners can help us stay on track, provide gentle reminders, and celebrate our successes along the way. This external support can boost our motivation and keep us committed to our goals, even when obstacles arise.

When building a support system, it is important to consider the unique needs and preferences of each individual. Some may prefer a small, intimate group, while others thrive in larger communities. The key is to surround yourself with individuals who genuinely care about your well-being and success. Remember, your support system should uplift you and contribute positively to your stress management journey.

In conclusion, finding support systems is an essential component of mastering stress management and setting realistic goals. They provide different perspectives, emotional support, and accountability, all of which contribute to making our goals more achievable. Take the time to identify and nurture your support system, for they can be the driving force behind your success. Remember, you are not alone on this journey, and with the right support, you can overcome any challenge that comes your way.

Maintaining a Positive Mindset

In our fast-paced and demanding world, stress has become an inevitable part of our lives. Whether it's work-related pressures, personal challenges, or societal expectations, stress can take a toll on our overall well-being. However, by mastering stress management, we can learn to navigate through life's challenges and maintain a positive mindset, enabling us to set and achieve realistic goals.

A positive mindset is the foundation for success in any aspect of life. It allows us to approach challenges with an optimistic attitude, believing in our abilities and focusing on solutions rather than problems. By cultivating a positive mindset, we can overcome obstacles, bounce back from setbacks, and stay motivated to reach our goals.

One of the first steps in maintaining a positive mindset is to practice self-awareness. Take time to understand your thoughts, emotions, and reactions to different situations. By recognizing negative thought patterns or self-limiting beliefs, you can challenge and reframe them into positive affirmations. This shift in thinking will empower you to view setbacks as opportunities for growth and learning.

Another essential aspect of maintaining a positive mindset is practicing gratitude. Take a moment each day to reflect on the things you are grateful for, no matter how small they may seem. Expressing gratitude helps shift your focus from what's going wrong to what's going right, fostering a positive outlook on life. It also cultivates resilience and helps you maintain perspective during challenging times.

Additionally, surround yourself with positive influences. Seek out supportive and like-minded individuals who inspire and motivate you. Engage in activities that bring you joy and boost your mood. By creating a positive environment, you are more likely to maintain a positive mindset and stay on track with your goals.

Lastly, self-care is crucial in maintaining a positive mindset. Prioritize activities that promote your physical, mental, and emotional well-being. Engage in regular exercise, practice mindfulness or meditation, and ensure you get enough restful sleep. By taking care of yourself, you are better equipped to handle stress and maintain a positive mindset.

In conclusion, maintaining a positive mindset is an essential component of mastering stress management and setting realistic goals. By practicing self-awareness, gratitude, surrounding yourself with positivity, and prioritizing self-care, you can cultivate a positive mindset that empowers you to overcome challenges and achieve your goals. Remember, a positive mindset is not about denying or avoiding negative emotions; it's about acknowledging them and choosing to focus on the positive aspects of life. Let positivity be your guiding light on your journey towards setting and achieving achievable goals.

Chapter 8: Building Resilience and Stress Coping Strategies

Developing Resilience Techniques

Resilience is the ability to bounce back from setbacks and challenges, and it plays a crucial role in managing stress and achieving our goals. In this subchapter, we will explore various techniques to develop resilience and strengthen our ability to handle stress effectively.

1. Cultivating a Growth Mindset: One of the first steps in developing resilience is adopting a growth mindset. This mindset sees challenges as opportunities for growth and learning rather than obstacles. By embracing a growth mindset, we can reframe setbacks as stepping stones to success, enabling us to persevere and remain focused on our goals.

2. Building a Support System: Surrounding ourselves with a strong support system is essential for developing resilience. Friends, family, and mentors can offer guidance, encouragement, and a listening ear during challenging times. Sharing our goals and progress with others not only helps us stay accountable but also provides a network of support when we face setbacks.

3. Practicing Self-Care: Taking care of ourselves physically, mentally, and emotionally is crucial for building resilience. Engaging in regular exercise, maintaining a healthy diet, and getting enough sleep can enhance our ability to cope with stress. Additionally, practicing mindfulness techniques such as meditation or deep breathing exercises can help us stay centered and calm in the face of adversity.

4. Developing Problem-Solving Skills: Resilient individuals are adept problem solvers. By enhancing our problem-solving skills, we can approach challenges with a proactive mindset. Analyzing the situation, brainstorming potential solutions, and taking decisive action can empower us to overcome obstacles and stay on track towards our goals.

5. Embracing Flexibility: Being flexible and adaptable is key to resilience. We must be willing to adjust our goals and strategies when necessary, as life is full of unexpected twists and turns. By embracing change and being open to new possibilities, we can navigate challenges more effectively and find alternative paths to success.

6. Learning from Failure: Failure is an inevitable part of life, and resilient individuals view it as an opportunity for growth. Instead of dwelling on past failures, we should analyze what went wrong and extract valuable lessons. By learning from our mistakes, we can make better decisions in the future and increase our chances of achieving our goals.

In conclusion, developing resilience techniques is vital for effectively managing stress and setting realistic goals. By cultivating a growth mindset, building a support system, practicing self-care, developing problem-solving skills, embracing flexibility, and learning from failure, we can enhance our resilience and overcome any obstacles that come our way. Remember, resilience is a skill that can be learned and strengthened over time, and it is the key to mastering stress management and achieving our goals.

Implementing Stress Coping Strategies

In today's fast-paced and demanding world, stress has become an integral part of our lives. It affects people from all walks of life, regardless of their age, profession, or background. The ability to cope with stress is crucial for maintaining overall well-being and achieving success in various aspects of life. In this subchapter, we will explore effective stress coping strategies that can be implemented by everyone, with a particular focus on individuals striving to set and achieve realistic goals.

1. Relaxation Techniques: Practicing relaxation techniques such as deep breathing exercises, meditation, yoga, or mindfulness can help reduce stress levels. These techniques enable individuals to attain a state of calmness and mental clarity, allowing them to approach their goals with a clear mind.

2. Time Management: One of the major stressors is feeling overwhelmed by a lack of time. By developing effective time management skills, individuals can prioritize their tasks and allocate sufficient time to work on their goals. This ensures that they are not burdened with excessive pressure, leading to a more stress-free approach towards goal attainment.

3. Physical Exercise: Engaging in regular physical exercise has proven to be an excellent stress management tool. Exercise releases endorphins, which are natural mood enhancers, reducing stress and promoting a positive mindset. Incorporating physical activity into your routine can boost energy levels and improve overall well-being, making goal setting and achievement more attainable.

4. Support Network: Building a strong support network is essential for managing stress effectively. Surrounding yourself with positive and understanding individuals who can offer guidance and encouragement can significantly alleviate stress levels. Sharing your goals and progress with your support network can provide motivation and accountability, making it easier to stay on track.

5. Self-Care: Practicing self-care is crucial for managing stress and maintaining a balanced life. Taking time for oneself, engaging in activities that bring joy and relaxation, and ensuring adequate rest and nutrition are all vital components of self-care. By prioritizing self-care, individuals can replenish their energy levels and approach their goals with renewed vigor and enthusiasm.

In conclusion, implementing stress coping strategies is essential for everyone, especially those striving to set and achieve realistic goals. By incorporating relaxation techniques, mastering time management, engaging in regular physical exercise, building a support network, and practicing self-care, individuals can effectively manage stress levels, maintain overall well-being, and enhance their chances of attaining their goals. Remember, stress is inevitable, but with the right coping strategies, it can be managed and even transformed into a catalyst for personal growth and success.

Seeking Professional Help When Needed

In the journey towards mastering stress management and setting realistic goals, there may come a time when seeking professional help becomes necessary. It is essential to understand that asking for assistance is not a sign of weakness, but rather a courageous step towards self-improvement. This subchapter aims to shed light on the importance of seeking professional help, the types of professionals available, and how they can support individuals in achieving their goals effectively.

Everyone faces unique challenges and situations in life, and sometimes these can become overwhelming. Whether it is managing stress, setting achievable goals, or dealing with personal issues, seeking professional help can provide invaluable guidance and support. Professionals such as therapists, counselors, life coaches, and mentors are trained to work with individuals to overcome obstacles and develop strategies for success.

Therapists and counselors specialize in helping individuals address emotional, mental, and psychological challenges. They provide a safe space for individuals to express their thoughts and feelings, offering guidance and techniques to manage stress effectively. These professionals can help identify underlying issues that may be hindering goal achievement and provide practical solutions to overcome them.

Life coaches are experts in goal setting and achievement. They work closely with individuals to define their goals, create action plans, and hold them accountable. By providing motivation, support, and guidance, life coaches can help individuals stay on track and overcome obstacles that may arise along the way.

Mentors, on the other hand, are experienced individuals who have achieved success in a particular field. They offer guidance, advice, and share their personal experiences to help others navigate their own journeys. Mentors can provide valuable insights and strategies for setting and achieving realistic goals based on their own expertise.

When seeking professional help, it is crucial to choose the right professional based on individual needs and preferences. Researching and finding a professional with the appropriate qualifications, experience, and a good fit with personal values and goals is essential for a successful outcome.

Remember, seeking professional help is a sign of strength and self-awareness. It demonstrates a willingness to learn, grow, and overcome challenges. By utilizing the support and expertise of professionals, individuals can enhance their stress management skills, set achievable goals, and ultimately lead more fulfilled lives. So, don't hesitate to reach out and seek the help you need to master stress management and achieve your goals.

Chapter 9: Balancing Goals and Self-Care

The Importance of Self-Care in Stress Management

In our fast-paced, demanding lives, stress has become an unavoidable part of our daily routine. Whether it's meeting deadlines at work, juggling personal relationships, or dealing with financial pressures, stress can take a toll on our mental and physical well-being. That's why it's essential to prioritize self-care as a crucial component of stress management.

Self-care refers to the intentional actions and practices we undertake to nurture our physical, emotional, and mental health. It involves recognizing our own needs and taking proactive steps to meet them. While it may seem counterintuitive to focus on ourselves when we're already overwhelmed, self-care is not selfish; rather, it is a vital investment in our overall well-being.

One of the primary reasons self-care is essential in stress management is that it helps us recharge and rejuvenate. When we neglect our own needs, we become depleted and more susceptible to stress. Engaging in activities that bring us joy and relaxation, such as exercise, hobbies, or spending time with loved ones, allows us to replenish our energy reserves and face challenges with a renewed sense of resilience.

Furthermore, self-care plays a crucial role in maintaining our physical health. Chronic stress can lead to a variety of health issues, including high blood pressure, heart disease, and weakened immune function. By prioritizing self-care, we can adopt healthy habits such as regular exercise, nutritious eating, and sufficient sleep, all of which boost our immune system and help us build physical resilience against stress.

Self-care also promotes emotional well-being. When we are under constant stress, our emotions can become overwhelming and difficult to manage. Engaging in activities that promote emotional well-being, such as journaling, practicing mindfulness, or seeking support from a therapist or support group, can help us process our emotions effectively and develop healthy coping mechanisms.

Lastly, self-care serves as a preventative measure against burnout. When we neglect our own needs for an extended period, we become more susceptible to burnout, a state of chronic exhaustion, cynicism, and reduced efficacy. By incorporating self-care practices into our daily routine, we can ward off burnout and maintain a healthy work-life balance.

In conclusion, self-care is an essential aspect of stress management. By prioritizing our own needs and engaging in activities that nurture our physical, emotional, and mental well-being, we can better navigate the challenges and demands of our lives. Remember, self-care is not selfish; it is an investment in our overall happiness and success. So, make self-care a priority and reap the benefits of a healthier, more balanced life.

Incorporating Self-Care Activities into Daily Routine

In today's fast-paced world, it is easy to get caught up in the never-ending demands of our daily lives. We often find ourselves juggling multiple responsibilities, striving to meet deadlines, and constantly trying to keep up with the ever-increasing pace of society. In this chaotic environment, it becomes crucial to prioritize self-care and incorporate it into our daily routines.

Self-care is not a luxury; it is a necessity for achieving overall well-being and maintaining a healthy work-life balance. It involves taking deliberate actions to nurture our physical, mental, and emotional health. By incorporating self-care activities into our daily routines, we can effectively manage stress and foster a sense of inner calm and fulfillment.

One way to incorporate self-care into our daily routines is by setting aside specific time slots for self-care activities. This could be as simple as dedicating 15 minutes each morning for meditation or yoga, or allocating an hour every evening for reading a book or engaging in a hobby. By consciously making time for self-care, we send a message to ourselves that our well-being matters and deserves attention.

Another way to incorporate self-care is by making small changes to our daily habits. This could involve prioritizing healthy eating by preparing nutritious meals, getting regular exercise, or ensuring we get enough sleep. Taking breaks during the workday to stretch or engage in deep breathing exercises can also go a long way in reducing stress and increasing productivity.

Additionally, it is important to identify activities that bring us joy and relaxation and incorporate them into our routines. This could include activities such as going for a walk in nature, listening to music, practicing mindfulness, or spending quality time with loved ones. Engaging in activities that bring us happiness and fulfillment replenishes our energy and helps us cope better with the challenges of daily life.

In conclusion, incorporating self-care activities into our daily routines is essential for maintaining a healthy work-life balance and managing stress. By setting aside specific time slots, making small changes to our habits, and engaging in activities that bring us joy, we can prioritize our well-being and nurture a positive mindset. Remember, self-care is not selfish; it is an investment in our overall health and happiness. So, make self-care a priority and watch as it transforms your life for the better.

Finding a Healthy Balance Between Goals and Well-being

In today's fast-paced world, it is easy to get caught up in the pursuit of our goals and forget about our overall well-being. We often prioritize our ambitions and aspirations over our mental, emotional, and physical health. However, it is crucial to find a healthy balance between our goals and well-being to lead a fulfilling and contented life.

Setting achievable goals is a fundamental aspect of personal growth and success. They provide us with direction, motivation, and a sense of purpose. However, it is equally important to recognize that our well-being should not be sacrificed in the process. Achieving goals should not come at the expense of our mental and physical health.

One key to finding a healthy balance between goals and well-being is to set realistic and manageable goals. It is essential to evaluate our capabilities, resources, and limitations before setting any objectives. Unrealistic goals can lead to stress, burnout, and disappointment. By setting achievable goals, we can ensure that our well-being is not compromised, and we can maintain a positive and healthy mindset throughout the journey.

Another crucial element is practicing self-care. Taking care of ourselves, both physically and mentally, is vital to achieving our goals effectively. Incorporating self-care activities into our daily routine, such as exercise, meditation, healthy eating, and quality sleep, can significantly enhance our overall well-being. It rejuvenates our energy levels, reduces stress, and improves our focus and productivity, making us better equipped to tackle our goals.

Additionally, it is crucial to develop a support system. Surrounding ourselves with positive and supportive individuals who believe in our goals can significantly impact our well-being. Sharing our aspirations and struggles with trusted friends, family, or mentors can provide us with emotional support, guidance, and motivation. Their encouragement can boost our confidence, help us overcome obstacles, and maintain a healthy balance between our goals and well-being.

Lastly, regular self-reflection is essential to assess our progress and make necessary adjustments. As we work towards our goals, it is crucial to check in with ourselves regularly. Are our goals still aligned with our values and aspirations? Are we neglecting our well-being in the pursuit of our goals? Regular self-reflection allows us to course-correct if needed and ensure that we are maintaining a healthy balance between our goals and overall well-being.

In conclusion, finding a healthy balance between goals and well-being is essential for a fulfilling and sustainable life. By setting realistic goals, practicing self-care, nurturing a support system, and engaging in regular self-reflection, we can achieve our goals while prioritizing our well-being. Remember, it is possible to achieve success without sacrificing our mental, emotional, and physical health.

Chapter 10: Sustaining Long-Term Success in Stress Management

Maintaining Consistency in Goal-Setting and Stress Management Practices

Consistency is the key to achieving success in any endeavor, especially when it comes to goal-setting and stress management. In this subchapter, we will explore the importance of maintaining consistency in these practices and provide practical tips for incorporating consistency into your daily routine.

Setting realistic and achievable goals is essential for personal and professional growth. However, many individuals struggle to stick to their goals and often find themselves overwhelmed with stress and anxiety. This is where consistency comes into play. By maintaining consistency in goal-setting, you create a framework that helps you stay focused, motivated, and on track.

One of the most effective ways to maintain consistency in goal-setting is by creating a daily routine. This routine should include dedicated time for goal reflection, planning, and action. By incorporating these activities into your daily schedule, you create a habit that becomes second nature over time. Consistently reviewing your goals and progress will keep them at the forefront of your mind, making it easier to stay committed and motivated.

Additionally, stress management is a critical component of achieving your goals. When stress levels are high, it becomes challenging to maintain focus and effectively work towards your objectives.

Consistency in stress management practices helps to reduce stress and maintain a balanced state of mind.

Implementing stress management techniques such as meditation, exercise, and time management into your daily routine can help you cope with stress more effectively. Consistently practicing these techniques will not only help you manage stress in the moment but also build resilience over time.

To maintain consistency in goal-setting and stress management practices, it is essential to create a support system. Surround yourself with individuals who share similar goals and values, as they can provide encouragement and hold you accountable. Consider joining a support group, finding a mentor, or partnering with a friend or colleague to ensure you stay consistent in your efforts.

In conclusion, maintaining consistency in goal-setting and stress management practices is crucial for achieving success and managing stress effectively. By creating a daily routine, practicing stress management techniques, and building a support system, you can stay on track and make steady progress towards your goals. Remember, consistency is the key to mastering stress management and setting realistic, achievable goals.

Evaluating and Adjusting Goals Over Time

Setting goals is an essential aspect of personal and professional growth. However, the journey towards achieving these goals is not always straightforward. Life is full of unexpected twists and turns that can throw us off track. Hence, it is crucial to learn how to evaluate and adjust our goals over time to ensure that they remain achievable and realistic.

Evaluation is the process of assessing the progress we have made towards our goals. It involves taking a step back, reflecting on our efforts, and identifying what has worked and what hasn't. By evaluating our goals, we can gain valuable insights into the areas where we need to make adjustments. This introspection allows us to understand our strengths and weaknesses, enabling us to make informed decisions about our next steps.

Adjusting goals is a necessary part of the goal-setting process. As circumstances change, we must be flexible and adaptable in our approach. Sometimes, external factors beyond our control may impact our ability to achieve our original goals. Adjusting these goals does not mean failure; rather, it is a sign of resilience and the willingness to adapt to new circumstances.

One of the key factors in evaluating and adjusting goals is self-awareness. We must be honest with ourselves about our abilities, limitations, and priorities. By understanding our strengths and weaknesses, we can set realistic expectations and adjust our goals accordingly. It is important to remember that setting unattainable goals will only lead to frustration and disappointment.

Regularly reviewing and adjusting goals is essential for long-term success. As we progress on our journey, we may realize that our original goals were too ambitious or not aligned with our current priorities. By evaluating and adjusting our goals, we can ensure that they remain relevant and meaningful.

To effectively evaluate and adjust goals over time, it is helpful to break them down into smaller, manageable milestones. This allows us to regularly assess our progress and make any necessary adjustments. Celebrating these milestones along the way can also provide motivation and encouragement to continue working towards our larger goals.

In conclusion, the process of evaluating and adjusting goals over time is a vital skill in mastering stress management and setting realistic goals. By regularly assessing our progress, being self-aware, and adapting to changing circumstances, we can ensure that our goals remain achievable and aligned with our aspirations. Remember, it is not about achieving perfection but rather making progress towards our ultimate objectives.

Celebrating and Reflecting on Personal Growth

In the journey of mastering stress management and setting realistic goals, it is crucial to take the time to celebrate and reflect on your personal growth. This subchapter emphasizes the importance of acknowledging and appreciating the progress you have made along the way, as well as the lessons learned from your experiences.

Personal growth is a continuous process that occurs as you strive to achieve your goals and overcome challenges. It is essential to recognize the milestones you have reached, regardless of their size or significance. By celebrating these achievements, you reinforce positive habits and boost your motivation to keep moving forward.

Celebration allows you to acknowledge the hard work, dedication, and perseverance you have invested in your journey. It serves as a reminder of your capabilities, helping to build confidence and self-belief. By taking the time to celebrate, you honor your progress and cultivate a positive mindset that can carry you through future obstacles.

Reflection is equally important in personal growth. It involves looking back on your experiences, assessing your actions, and extracting valuable lessons. Reflecting allows you to gain insights into your strengths and weaknesses, enabling you to make more informed decisions going forward. It also helps you identify areas for improvement and provides an opportunity to set new goals that align with your evolving aspirations.

Taking the time to celebrate and reflect on your personal growth is not only beneficial for your mental and emotional well-being but also for setting achievable goals. By understanding how far you have come, you gain a clearer perspective on what is realistic and attainable for the future. It helps you set goals that are challenging yet attainable, ensuring a sense of fulfillment and avoiding unnecessary stress.

Remember that personal growth is not a linear process, and setbacks are a natural part of it. Celebrating and reflecting on your growth allows you to acknowledge these setbacks as opportunities for learning and growth rather than as failures. It helps you maintain a growth mindset, embracing challenges as stepping stones toward your ultimate success.

In conclusion, celebrating and reflecting on personal growth is an essential aspect of mastering stress management and setting realistic goals. By taking the time to celebrate your achievements and reflect on your experiences, you cultivate a positive mindset, gain valuable insights, and set yourself up for continued growth and success.

Conclusion: Embracing a Stress-Free Future

In today's fast-paced and demanding world, stress has become an inevitable part of our lives. We constantly find ourselves juggling multiple responsibilities, striving to meet deadlines, and trying to achieve our goals. However, the key to managing stress lies in setting realistic and achievable goals. In this book, "Mastering Stress Management: The Art of Setting Realistic Goals," we have explored various strategies and techniques to help you navigate through the stress-inducing challenges and embrace a stress-free future.

Throughout this journey, we have learned the importance of setting achievable goals. Many of us fall into the trap of setting unrealistic expectations for ourselves, leading to frustration, burnout, and increased stress levels. By understanding the principles of goal setting, we can create a roadmap that aligns with our capabilities and resources, enabling us to make steady progress towards our objectives.

One of the fundamental aspects of setting achievable goals is to prioritize and focus on what truly matters. Often, we get overwhelmed by the sheer number of tasks and responsibilities that come our way. By identifying our core values and aligning our goals accordingly, we can streamline our efforts and direct our energy towards what brings us joy and fulfillment.

Another vital strategy we have discussed is the power of breaking down our goals into smaller, manageable steps. This approach allows us to make consistent progress, celebrate small victories, and maintain momentum. By dividing our larger goals into achievable milestones, we can overcome procrastination, gain a sense of accomplishment, and reduce stress associated with overwhelming tasks.

Furthermore, we have explored the significance of self-care and stress management techniques. Taking care of our physical, mental, and emotional well-being is essential for maintaining balance and resilience in the face of stress. From mindfulness practices to regular exercise and healthy lifestyle choices, we have learned how to nurture ourselves and build a strong foundation for stress-free living.

In conclusion, "Mastering Stress Management: The Art of Setting Realistic Goals" provides a comprehensive guide to help EVERY ONE, regardless of their background or niche, navigate the complexities of goal setting and embrace a stress-free future. By implementing the strategies and techniques outlined in this book, you will be equipped with the necessary tools to set achievable goals, prioritize effectively, and manage stress in a sustainable way. Remember, the journey towards a stress-free future begins with a commitment to self-care and a willingness to embrace realistic goals. Start your journey today and unlock the potential for a happier and more fulfilling life.